CLASSICAL RIDING

Johanna Sharples

Illustrations by
Carole Vincer

KENILWORTH PRESS

First published in the UK by
Kenilworth Press, an imprint of Quiller Publishing Ltd

British Library Cataloguing in Publication Data
A catalogue record for this book is available from the British Library

ISBN 978-1-905693-19-1
Printed in China

Disclaimer of Liability
The author and publisher shall have neither liability nor
responsibility to any person or entity with respect to any loss or
damage caused or alleged to be caused directly or indirectly by the
information contained in this book. While the book is as accurate as
the author can make it, there may be errors, omissions and
inaccuracies.

KENILWORTH PRESS
An imprint of Quiller Publishing Ltd
Wykey House, Wykey, Shrewsbury, SY4 1JA
tel: 01939 261616 fax: 01939 261606
e-mail: info@quillerbooks.com
website: www.kenilworthpress.co.uk

Contents

INTRODUCTION

What is classical horsemanship, why should you use it, and how does it differ from other horse-training methods?

Just as many roads lead to Rome, there are many routes open to those interested in training horses. Careful route-planning is the essential first step for any successful journey, and for thousands of years the knowledge and experience of the great masters of horsemanship have been used to set standards and provide points of reference to guide riders in the right direction. This system is recognised as classical horsemanship.

The days of the classical riding academy, where the theory and practice of correct horsemanship were taught and developed over many years, have virtually disappeared, with a few notable exceptions such as the Spanish Riding School of Vienna. However, we can still become classical horsemen by practising classical techniques with our horses, and proving their efficacy to ourselves and to others by the results we achieve.

It is said that haste is the enemy of true art, and indeed some may find the classical route to a trained horse is not necessarily the shortest. Gadgets, short cuts and quick fixes are not on the agenda; the classical horseman believes that it is better to take a little longer on a smoother road if that means reaching the destination with a sound and happy horse.

Some argue that the horse doesn't need to be happy to be well trained. In classical terms, the two are inseparable; it is essential to appreciate the strong connection between the psychological needs of the horse and his physical performance, because the horse's state of mind and willingness to learn are crucial factors in the success of his training.

It's also much easier to teach a content, confident and willing pupil. But while you are indeed your horse's teacher, he is also yours, and another characteristic of the classical student's mind-set is humility and respect for the horse. However experienced or talented the rider, there is always more to learn. Your horse will be living proof of your success; he will reflect your strengths and your weaknesses. The true classical horseman will use this knowledge to improve not only his horse, but himself.

Classical horsemanship

- Uses humane and effective techniques developed from the knowledge and experience of old equestrian masters and proven over many years.

- Is a logical, steady and natural progression appropriate to the horse's age, ability and stage of training, without the need for, or use of, fear, force or gadgets.

- Aims for the contentment, confidence, health and longevity of the horse by using gymnastically correct and psychologically appropriate exercises.

- Suits the majority of horses most of the time, and allows for the strengths and weaknesses of each individual regardless of breed, size, type or talent.

- Respects the needs of the horse above the ambitions of the rider.

THE CLASSICALLY TRAINED RIDER

The classically trained rider

Anyone who has had a riding lesson, from a classical trainer or not, will hopefully have come away with the impression that sitting in the 'right place' on a horse's back is important. For classical horsemen, the rider's seat and position in the saddle is fundamental because how you use your body directly affects the horse's ability to use his.

Classical riding is not just about the rider giving aids and the horse obeying them; it's about enjoying a subtle two-way conversation where you are 'listening' to the horse with your body and being very aware of how every move you make means something to him. An incorrect way of riding will also impair the horse's movement and athletic ability and over a period of time, it can lead to unsoundness in the horse and discomfort for the rider.

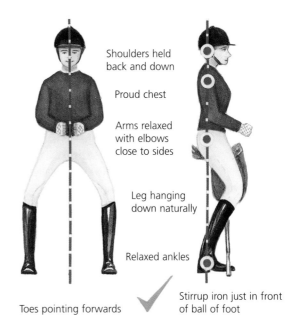

Shoulders held back and down

Proud chest

Arms relaxed with elbows close to sides

Leg hanging down naturally

Relaxed ankles

Toes pointing forwards

Stirrup iron just in front of ball of foot

SOME COMMON FAULTS OF A BAD SEAT

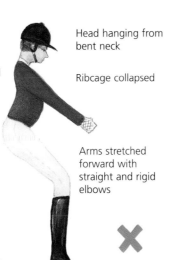

Rounded shoulders

Stiff back

Hips rocking forward to create a hollow lower back, or jamming backwards to flatten the lower back are equally wrong, the lower back should be in a neutral (upright and stable) position

Buttocks pressed back towards cantle

Crotch pressed down and rider perched

Head hanging from bent neck

Ribcage collapsed

Arms stretched forward with straight and rigid elbows

What do we mean by a correct classical seat?

In a classical riding context, 'seat' includes not just the buttocks but the seat bones, pubic arch, thighs and even, some would say, the lower back and abdominal muscles. The idea is to create a stable platform from which you can give precise aids – aids which really 'aid' or help the horse to understand and carry out what is being asked.

What is the effect of a bad seat on a horse?

If your weight is on your buttocks and your legs are forward, and you are balancing yourself with the reins, the horse will hollow his back away from the discomfort your seat is causing. He may also throw his head in the air, hold his breath and retract his ribcage from contact with your legs, all of which are the opposite of what you are trying to achieve.

Why is a classically correct seat so important?

The connection between the seat of the rider and the carriage of the horse are absolutely inseparable; one can either facilitate or sabotage the other. The classical rider therefore places great emphasis on developing a correct seat above all else. Riders of the Spanish Riding School and similar institutions spend years perfecting their seat, many of them on the lunge, hence the impression of absolute unity you may notice in a classical display by a team trained in this way. Not only are the riders pretty much identical in their positions, but their horses maintain very similar outlines as a result.

The pelvis and its surrounding muscles form the core of the classical rider's position, and by learning to manipulate the angle of the pelvis the rider can exert very subtle control over the horse's movement. For example, by flattening the back (tilting the pelvis backward), the horse can be allowed forward into a more extended pace. Likewise, by enhancing the curve in the lower back (tilting the pelvis forward), the horse can be gathered into a more collected pace, as the seat will act as a restraining aid.

Subtle shifting of weight between the seat bones also influences the direction in which the horse travels, particularly when asking for sideways or 'lateral' movement.

A common mistake when trying to use the seat bones is to simply collapse the hip or shift the entire bodyweight to one side. This compromises your position and will not help the horse. Rather than trying to put weight onto one particular seat bone, you may find it easier to lift the weight from the other – the natural effect will be the same without compromising your position.

Rider with collapsed right hip

Rider sitting too far to the right

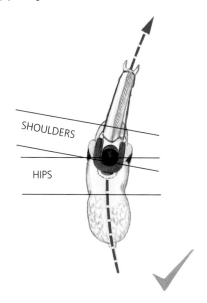

SHOULDERS

HIPS

The rider's shoulders and hips must be aligned with those of the horse

Riding curves, turns and sideways movement
When a horse is going in a straight line the rider should sit centrally and straight. On a curve, turn or circle, the shoulders and hips turn slightly in the direction of the movement to bring more weight onto the inner seat bone. In this way the **whole body** is involved in turning the horse. It is important not to use just the hands to turn a horse by pulling the rein, as this will result in him only bending the neck round (see page 13 for examples of incorrect bending). Keep the elbows lightly 'anchored' to the sides to prevent you throwing your hand forward and to ensure you are using your shoulders correctly to make the turn, not just the hand and arm.

ABDOMINAL AND THIGH MUSCLES

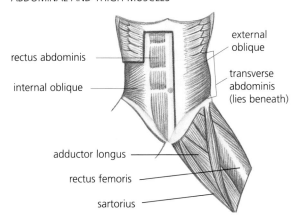

rectus abdominis

internal oblique

external oblique

transverse abdominis (lies beneath)

adductor longus

rectus femoris

sartorius

Keeping a balanced position is easy enough until the horse moves! A stiff body on top of a moving or bouncing body will cause jarring and banging. The human body enjoys a natural flexibility and elasticity that allow it to act as a shock absorber and move in union with the horse using the thigh and back muscles. The natural 'corset' of muscles (shown above) around the lower back and abdomen give the body what is known as 'core stability', which is important for absorbing movement as it allows the pelvis to rotate and absorb the motion of the horse and adopt the proper angles as the horse moves.

EXERCISES

Finding your seat
1. Mount and remove both feet from the stirrups. Sit erect, drawing the back of your neck upwards, then take the thighs away from the saddle and draw your knees up, out and back, rotating from the hips as if to draw a small circle with each knee (clockwise with left knee, anticlockwise with right knee). Relax and ease your toes back into the stirrups without disturbing the deep, broad contact your seat and thighs now have with the saddle. If your stirrups are too short, they may force the leg forward and cause you to brace the knee and ankle, so lengthen the stirrups as necessary to prevent this.

2. Take each foot out of the stirrups, bend your knee and take hold of the front of your ankle, pressing the knee backwards and heel up towards your buttocks. You should feel a strong stretch down the front of your thigh as the front of the hip opens and the pelvis becomes more upright. Hold your leg in this position for a few seconds, then slowly drop it. This should place your leg in an almost straight position. Relax your leg so it is slightly bent at the knee, not stretched uncomfortably straight. Your stirrups should be just long enough to rest the balls of your feet higher then your heels, without the heels jamming down, giving stability yet flexibility to the legs.

3. Balance check. Finding out more about how you use (or misuse!) your own body off the horse will give you valuable feedback about how you use it on the horse, and help you to improve as a rider. Can you lift one leg and maintain postural alignment? Which side do you find easier? Do you feel yourself collapsing into one hip in order to stay upright? Like your horse, you are naturally one-sided, and this feedback is important when it comes to analysing and improving ridden problems.

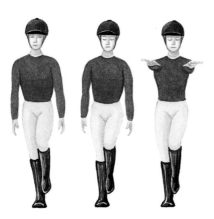

Tips for classical positioning

- Relax your face, lips and jaw muscles. It has an amazing effect on the rest of your body!

- Relax the buttocks and make them as broad as possible.

- Allow the arms to sink downwards in a casual way, with elbows held into the sides to help give stability to the arm and hand without tension.

- Think of keeping softly closed fingers, making a flat-fingered but **not** tightly clenched fist.

- A common fault is drawing the hand back into the stomach; to avoid pulling backwards or restrictly the horse's forward movement, keep your hand forward. It may help to imagine pressing your navel forwards towards your wrists, but without hollowing the back.

- Legs should be draped around the horse's sides, not gripping them.

- Forcing your weight down into the stirrup causes unwanted tension in the knee and ankle, and forces your seat up and out of contact with the saddle. Lengthen your stirrup leathers to a point where your toe is supported lightly in the iron, and without locking out at the knee (think 'toe up' rather than 'heel down').

THE CLASSICALLY TRAINED HORSE

The classically trained horse: what does he look like?

When drawing or imagining our dream horse he is probably well muscled and prances lightly along with a beautifully arched neck. Never does our dream horse drag himself along with a hollow back, open mouth and head stuck in the air, swishing his tail and putting his ears back in response to our aids!

The reason why there is such a difference between the horse of our dreams and the horse of our reality is that we are training him incorrectly. The aim of classical training techniques is to develop the self-carriage which is the key to unleashing the proud, prancing equine within every horse!

The classical position for horses

Like the rider, there is an ideal body position which every horse must maintain in order to develop self-carriage. This is the ability to remain strong, balanced, effective and beautiful in motion, even under the weight of a rider; the most advanced form of self-carriage is known as 'collection' and is physically very demanding for the horse.

It is achieved by using a series of body-building and balancing exercises which help the horse discover how to use his body most easily and effectively, and to develop the muscles he needs to do it. This is the purpose of so-called 'schooling exercises', and some of the most useful are described later in this book.

This 'body-building' or self-carriage development must be done in a logical, progressive sequence, however – hence the classical training pyramid which follows. Forcing the back end to 'come under' before the muscles are strong enough to cope, or

pulling the head and neck into a 'pretty' position using force or mechanical gadgets will cause physical damage and incorrect development, which may take years to remedy. Experts in equine biomechanics estimate that it takes a minimum of two years for the chain of muscles necessary for a more collected outline to stabilise and develop. This is why classical riders do not believe in short cuts – none have yet been discovered which are not to the detriment of the horse's correct development.

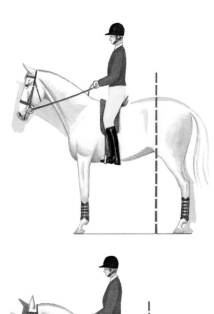

Correct training encourages the horse to adjust his posture in order to carry himself and his rider with greater ease

9

Equine core stability

Like his rider, the horse's ability to achieve and maintain a correct position depends partly on the strength and stability of his 'mid-section', i.e. his abdominal, side and back muscles. Once this part of him is strong, he can support his swinging back even with a rider, and naturally extend his neck forwards and downwards, bringing his hind legs underneath him to keep his balance. As he tucks his pelvis under, so the muscles become even stronger, and able to support the horse as he takes weight on his hind legs. One consequence of taking more weight on the haunches is that they lower and the forehand becomes relatively higher and lighter. The horse raises his neck from the withers into an arch with the poll the highest point and his nose on or just in front of the vertical.

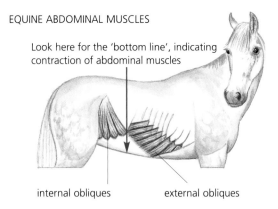

EQUINE ABDOMINAL MUSCLES

Look here for the 'bottom line', indicating contraction of abdominal muscles

internal obliques   external obliques

For a horse to engage correctly, the abdominal muscles must contract to elevate the back. Look for a visible line or ridge running along the bottom of the ribs. This is often referred to as the 'bottom line' and is just as important as the 'top line' (of the back and neck) when it comes to engagement.

Remember: the classical rider's seat and position are fundamental because how you use your body directly affects the horse's ability to use his. Your horse's 'position' reflects yours, and vice versa.

The joints of the horse and rider work together; the rider's seat bones can affect the horse's ability to use his back and the joints of his hind legs correctly

When the heel of the rider gives an aid it stimulates the horse to use his abdominal muscles, rather like someone poking you in the stomach – your natural reaction is to contract the stomach muscles and arch your back away. When the horse lifts his back, it changes the position of his pelvis and allows the hind legs to step further beneath him.

Horse and rider share a 'cycle' of energy generated by the rider's seat and legs, which activate the horse's hindquarters. The flow of energy can be blocked at any time if the rider's hips, knees or ankles stiffen against it.

THE CLASSICAL TRAINING PYRAMID

In rhythm.

Creating self-carriage using the classical training pyramid

The main aim of classical horsemanship is to develop a horse gymnastically so that he is capable of carrying himself and his rider in the most effective way. The gymnastic ideal is a horse in self-carriage; the highest degree of self-carriage is known as collection. A horse capable of true and sustained collection is considered to be very advanced in his training.

Collection is not achieved by trying to ride the horse in a collected frame every day, however. The horse's ability to collect is built up over many years using gymnastically correct exercises within a logical training structure. The classical training pyramid described here provides a good visual image of this structure. It has been developed over many years using the combined wisdom of classical trainers, and involves six steps or levels of training which must be followed in order, so that the horse is properly prepared to advance successfully to the next step.

 1 Rhythm

Like a metronome beating out time, the horse's footfalls at each gait must stay in a steady and regular rhythm. Relaxation is essential for good rhythm; a tense horse will take quick, short and often irregular steps.

When the horse is physically and mentally relaxed, he should step naturally to the rhythm of the natural gaits: the walk is a four-beat movement, the trot two-beat, the canter three-beat, and the rein-back two-beat. Like learning a dance, the more slowly the horse steps the easier it is for him to develop coordination, which is why new exercises are usually taught in walk. Loss of rhythm may be a sign that the horse is finding an exercise difficult.

 2 Suppleness

This is the looseness and flexibility of the horse's body. To perform schooling exercises with ease and develop self-carriage, he needs to be supple in two ways. **Longitudinal** suppleness involves the muscles of the horse's haunches, back, neck, poll, and jaw, giving him the ability to lift his back and swing forward. **Lateral** suppleness is the degree to which a horse can bend his body and neck from side to side, such as on a circle or to move sideways. Most horses are less laterally supple one way than the other, just as humans are left- or right-handed. Lack of lateral suppleness will often show as crookedness on a circle (see point 5, Straightness).

11

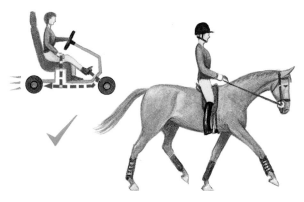

A horse who will not accept the rider's contact is like revving the engine of a car that is not in gear! When the horse is accepting the rider's hands, seat and legs, he is 'in gear' and ready for action.

How far the horse steps the hind legs underneath his barrel, rather than having them trail behind, can be an indication of impulsion. The horse with hind legs well beneath him is ready and primed for action.

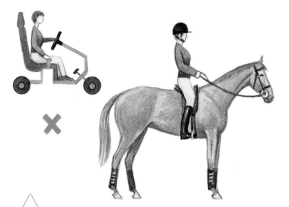

 3 Contact

Good contact is when the horse accepts and responds to seat and leg aids while maintaining a round outline with a mouth that is relaxed and accepting the bit. The power generated by his 'engine' (the hindquarters) can be contained and directed. Contact is not established by the rider's hand gripping the horse's mouth, but by the horse coming up into the rider's hand, lifting and driving himself forward from the back to the front. A sign of good contact is when the horse's back is raised, his quarters engaged, his poll the highest point, his jaw relaxed, and his nose a hint in front of the vertical.

 4 Impulsion

This is the amount of free-flowing fuel or energy you have contained within the system, so that when you ease the brake and put your foot on the accelerator, something actually happens! Impulsion causes a 'power surge' of forward movement and allows the horse's back to swing, his quarters to engage and his forelegs to articulate. Good impulsion is apparent in a horse who appears to have an innate desire to go forward with active, lively steps, rather than having to be pushed all the time.

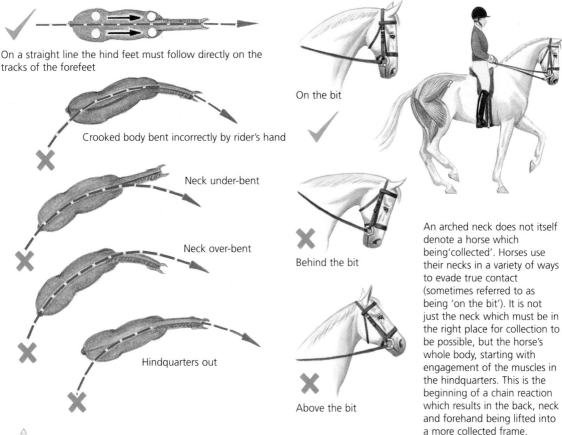

On a straight line the hind feet must follow directly on the tracks of the forefeet

Crooked body bent incorrectly by rider's hand

Neck under-bent

Neck over-bent

Hindquarters out

On the bit

Behind the bit

Above the bit

An arched neck does not itself denote a horse which being 'collected'. Horses use their necks in a variety of ways to evade true contact (sometimes referred to as being 'on the bit'). It is not just the neck which must be in the right place for collection to be possible, but the horse's whole body, starting with engagement of the muscles in the hindquarters. This is the beginning of a chain reaction which results in the back, neck and forehand being lifted into a more collected frame.

 5 Straightness

Horses are naturally crooked and favour one side over the other. We can straighten them using exercises to develop muscles as evenly as possible on both sides, and by doing an equal number of exercises on each rein. Crookedness is caused by uneven lateral suppleness (i.e. one side is stiffer than the other) and one hind leg being weaker than the other, which is why, ironically, a good test for straightness is to ride a circle! A horse will show his precise area of weakness by under- or over-bending through his neck, back or quarters as shown above. A horse is truly straight when the hind foot steps in the line of the front foot.

 6 Collection

Only when the previous five stages have been consolidated is the ultimate goal of collection possible. Collection involves the lowering of the croup, lightness of the forehand and shorter, higher steps, giving a more defined moment of suspension in the air. Collection is possible in the walk, trot and canter, and is achieved and tested using more advanced exercises such as those shown on pages 20–23. A horse in collection feels as if he will maintain all of the above – rhythm, suppleness, contact, impulsion and straightness – without interference from the rider. This is a horse in true self-carriage.

GROUNDWORK: IN-HAND BASICS

So, where do you start 'hands on' training? In the same place as all great classical trainers over the centuries of course, and that is from the ground. Classical *horsemanship*, rather just *riding*, implies a complete training system of which riding the horse is only a part. Although the art of working horses from the ground is often forgotten these days, groundwork is a fundamental part of classical training. It merits a lengthy training book in its own right, but just to give you an idea, some of the activities which will help your horse's gymnastic development besides riding include in-hand work in a cavesson or bridle, single-rein lungeing and work on two reins (long-reining and two-rein lungeing).

Getting started

Working a horse in hand on the most basic level involves gaining multi-directional control of his body; he must learns to stop, go forward, go backwards and move his shoulders and haunches in response to your aids.

Because you are on the ground beside him, the horse gets his aids from your body language and positioning, along with touches from the whip in the place where you would normally give a ridden aid to direct him. It's really no different from getting him to move over when you are in the stable, or manoeuvre around other horses and through a tricky gate coming in from the field, for example.

The whip is held like a conductor's baton and used with precision and delicacy. It is your main aid when working the horse from the ground; other aids include your voice, body position and body language.

Groundwork

- Teaches the kind of obedience, comprehension and gymnastic development which builds firm foundations for ridden work.

- Prevents a less experienced rider from hindering the horse while both are learning.

- Adds interest and variety to a training programme.

- Is the perfect way to warm up and supple a horse before riding.

- Allows the handler to observe closely how the horse is using his body without the influence of a rider.

Start by using a correctly fitted cavesson, preferably a solid leather type, with an ordinary leadrope attached. The noseband and cheek strap must be firmly fitted, unlike with the bridle, since in this case they have a stabilising function. The cavesson makes it possible to exert control without having to pull at the mouth.

When the horse is obedient in the cavesson, greater finesse and control over bend can be achieved using a bridle, with the reins held as shown – one hand a few inches (several cms) from the horse's mouth by the bit, the other by his shoulder. This hand also carries the whip.

GROUNDWORK: EARLY EXERCISES TO PRACTISE

Caress the horse all over with gentle strokes from the whip

Familiarise the horse with the whip The whip is to correct, reward, explain or even reassure the horse – never to punish. The horse must develop trust in the whip and the hand which wields it; this will be destroyed if it is used brutally.

Move the horse's back end (haunches) by asking the front end to 'halt' using the cavesson and leadrope and touching the whip in the girth area, where your leg would give the aid in ridden work.

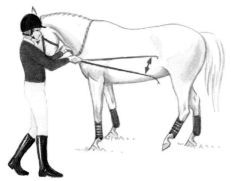

Move the horse backwards Stand alongside your horse's shoulder facing backwards, and move forward yourself as you gently fan the whip up and down along the horse's side but without actually touching him.

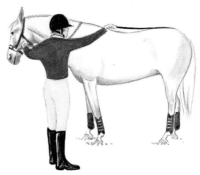

Halt Use the verbal command as you exert pressure on the leadrope and lay the whip lightly across the horse's loins.

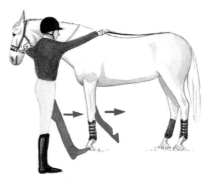

Move the horse's front end (shoulders) by lying the whip across the horse's loins to ask for 'halt' from the haunches, then walking towards and into the horse's shoulder, exerting gentle pressure from a hand on the side of the face if necessary to push him away from you.

Move the horse sideways by putting the shoulder-moving exercise together with the haunches exercise. Ask for one step sideways from the front legs, then one step sideways from the hind legs to straighten up – rather like moving a fridge or heavy box where you wiggle one end then the other to make progress. Gradually the steps will flow together in one continuous sideways movement.

Using the voice Using verbal commands during ground-work sessions will improve your horse's vocabulary in preparation for obedience at distance, such as on the lunge. Sometimes saying things out loud to your horse can clarify exactly what you are asking for in your own mind too!

GROUNDWORK: DISTANCE LEARNING

LUNGEING

This is one of the most commonly used and frequently abused forms of training and exercising a horse. Sending a horse round and round in circles contributes nothing towards the goal of collection unless done constructively and with the aim of stimulating the horse's mind and body, as one might in a ridden schooling session. Challenge your horse with frequent changes of rein, circle size and transitions, and by insisting on instant obedience to verbal commands.

Lungeing equipment

Without the influence of a rider, the true state of the horse's self-carriage can be seen, and it's not always a pretty sight! No wonder that lungers are often the worst offenders when it comes to gadgets. A horse in a correct outline should be a consequence of correct work, not simply a result of mechanical pressure, so restrict yourself to side reins attached to the snaffle rings on each side and buckled to the girth. Every time your horse evades you by opening his mouth, tossing his head or similar displays of discomfort, he is telling you something useful about your riding and training. Classical trainers welcome such feedback from the horse and use it to check correct progress. If you want to learn, then don't silence your greatest teacher!

COMMUNICATION ON THE LUNGE

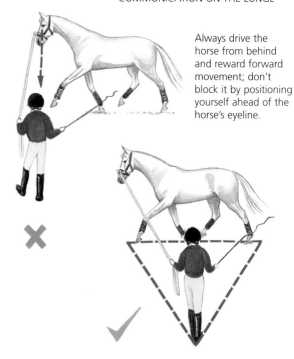

Always drive the horse from behind and reward forward movement; don't block it by positioning yourself ahead of the horse's eyeline.

Body language and positioning are important when lungeing. When viewed from above, a triangle should be formed by the lunger, whip and horse.

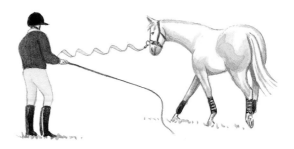

Shaking (or 'snaking') the lunge line at the horse is a useful technique if he is pulling or leaning on it; it is the distance learning equivalent of a ridden half-halt, so helps to establish contact and gain the horse's attention before giving a command, and can enforce the command to halt.

TWO-REIN LUNGEING

Using two separate lunge lines requires practice but the results are well worth it. If you can ride a bicycle or drive a car then you have all the coordination you need to succeed! Two-rein lungeing helps you to develop the 'feel' for the contact you will need when riding. You can use the reins as if 'riding' your horse from the ground, encouraging him to step into the outside rein, and soften into the inside rein. The line around the back encourages a greater 'tucking under' of the haunches and allows the horse to lift his forehand correctly.

If you haven't got a special lungeing roller or want to use this as a warm-up before riding, you can adapt your usual tack for two-rein lungeing like this:
1. Twist the reins out of the way and secure with the throat lash.
2. Let the stirrups down and secure them to each other beneath horse's girth using an old stirrup leather or similar.
3. Feed the clip end of lunge line through the stirrup and clip the lunge rein to bit ring. Repeat on other side with second lunge rein.

ABC OF TURNING HORSE ON ON TWO REINS

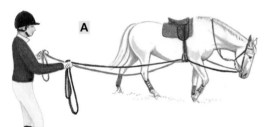

A First, use two different coloured lunge reins so you know which is which! Drop the contact on the inside rein so it is loose enough to allow the horse to turn but not to trail on the floor.

B Start to walk briskly in the other direction while reeling in the slack and taking up contact on the outside rein. Your horse should read your body language and start to turn.

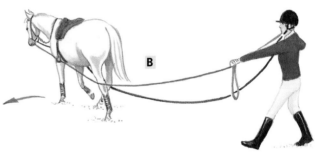

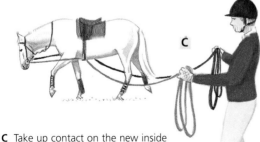

C Take up contact on the new inside rein and send the horse forward in the new direction.

LONG-REINING

This differs from two-rein lungeing in that the handler walks closely beside the horse's hindquarters and exerts a more 'rider-like' influence. It is a good 'training test' as the horse must perform most gaits and school movements at the sedate walking pace of the handler, even in canter. This encourages activity and impulsion rather than speed, an increased articulation of the joints and elevation of the stride, giving greater 'lift' and engagement of the quarters.

RIDDEN EXERCISES: NOVICE

As explained, the horse's ability to assume and maintain a collected outline is built up over time using specific exercises, first done individually, and then put together as a more challenging gymnastic sequence in a comprehensive schooling programme.

It is wise to familiarise yourself with as many exercises as possible so that you are equipped to deal with a variety of different horses and situations. You should also have a written plan of what you intend to achieve with your schooling in both the short and the long term, to give your training structure and coherence on a daily, monthly and even annual basis.

Here are some useful exercises which form the core of most schooling programmes.

1. Bending

Since straightness is one of your training goals, start by bending! (See page 13, the classical training pyramid.) Through bending, the horse is elasticised, and his stiff areas loosened up, making it possible for him to move straight. Bending is also a kind of one-sided or 'unilateral' collection, since during a turn the horse must flex and use the inside hock more than the outside. It is therefore an important building block in producing the ultimate goal of true 'bilateral' collection, where both hocks must be more deeply flexed and active together.

Circles are based upon bending, which is why most school movements are made up of them in one form or another. Riding curved lines strengthens the inside hind leg in preparation for greater collection, helps the horse engage and find his balance and stretches the outside of the horse to develop lateral suppleness.

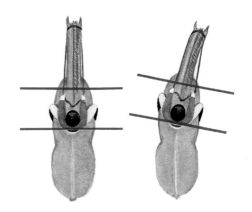

The rider doesn't physically bend the horse. It's the way you sit and the school patterns you use that cause the bend. Using the reins to turn the horse will result only in bending the neck; to bend and turn the horse's whole body in a smooth arc you must turn your shoulders and follow the movement. Imagine you have a spotlight in the middle of your chest which you need to shine in the direction of travel.

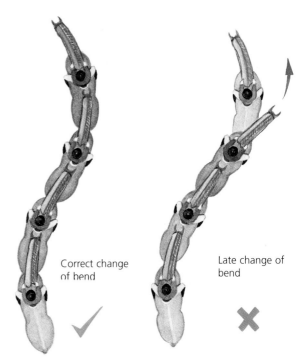

Correct change of bend

Late change of bend

Approach the change of bend as if it were a transition, requiring accuracy and preparation. Fix real or imaginary markers and start to turn your shoulders the stride before, otherwise you will end up making a late change of bend.

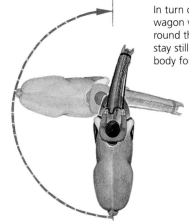

In turn on the forehand, imagine a wagon wheel: the hind legs step round the rim, while the forelegs stay still as the hub, and the horse's body forms a wheel spoke.

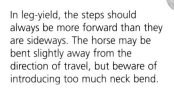

In leg-yield, the steps should always be more forward than they are sideways. The horse may be bent slightly away from the direction of travel, but beware of introducing too much neck bend.

2. Turn on the forehand

At first a horse must learn to understand yielding to the leg (i.e. stepping away sideways in response to a leg aid) when at a standstill, which is why turn on the forehand is usually one of the first lateral (or side-stepping) exercises to be taught. From the rider's point of view, it is the beginning of learning how to use one leg aid independently of the other to give a lateral aid. From a square halt, the horse is asked to move his quarters away from the rider's leg to step around his forehand, which should stay on the same spot.

3. Leg yield

The leg-yield involves forward and sideways stepping. It is useful preparation for further lateral work and increases the horse's understanding of sideways movement, this time while on the move. Performed correctly it encourages engagement of the hindquarters, improves the natural balance of the horse and requires greater control and coordination from the rider in preparation for more complex movements later on, and is usually done in walk and trot.

4. Transitions

Transitions are a good test of your training, because to do them correctly a horse needs to use his haunches well. Using them extensively during schooling sessions will keep your horse supple, submissive and attentive. They are also an indication of the level you are working at. Initially transitions are progressive between gaits, such as from walk to trot, trot to canter. Direct transitions, such as going directly from walk to canter, require a greater degree of collection and concentration (especially true of downward transitions). You can also do transitions within the same gait by lengthening or shortening the stride, such as from working to medium trot.

RIDDEN EXERCISES: INTERMEDIATE

Learning to manoeuvre the front and back end of the horse independently of each other is important for control and straightening. For example, it gives the rider the ability to move the shoulders back in front of the hindquarters when they stray, like gaining control of a wobbly supermarket trolley!

The rider can break down the early requirements by simply asking the horse first to move either his shoulders or his hips sideways to the inside or the outside of the track (i.e. shoulder-in/out and haunches-in/out). As a general rule, bending away from the direction of travel is easier for the horse than bending into the direction of travel.

1. Shoulder-in

Shoulder-in is excellent for teaching the rider to straighten the horse. To be strictly correct in competition, the horse should be on three tracks (i.e. three lines of parallel hoofprints when viewed from directly in front or behind), but any lesser degree of angle is a good start and still has gymnastic benefit when schooling at home. Because the horse is made to curve his body round in front of the inside hind leg, this leg is obliged to carry more weight as it is the prime mover for propelling the horse along, so shoulder-in also helps the horse on his journey into collection and self-carriage by strengthening the inside hind leg. A common mistake is to allow the shoulder-in to become simply 'head and neck-in', which has little gymnastic value.

2. Haunches-in

Step one in gaining control of the quarters is to ask the horse to bend his body so that his haunches come off the track, while he

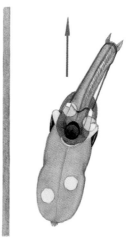

SHOULDER-IN

In shoulder-in the horse is moving forward but at an angle (approximately 30 degrees away from the track), looking away from the direction in which he is moving. The whole body should be curved to make the inside hind leg carry weight and propel the horse along. The rider's inside hand, leg and seat bone ask for slight bend.

HAUNCHES-IN

Haunches-in to the left: the left rein asks for slight bend while the haunches yield to the right leg and come off the track so that the horse is walking forwards at an angle.

continues walking forwards at an angle. This is the first exercise where he is required to bend into the direction of travel, i.e. looking the way he is going, rather than being bent away from it. As with shoulder-in, a lesser angle is sufficient for beginners; at the start you may also keep the head and neck straight while you get the feel of moving the quarters, adding flexion later on when the horse is ready. Haunches-in done along three equal tracks is a competition movement, known as travers (see page 22).

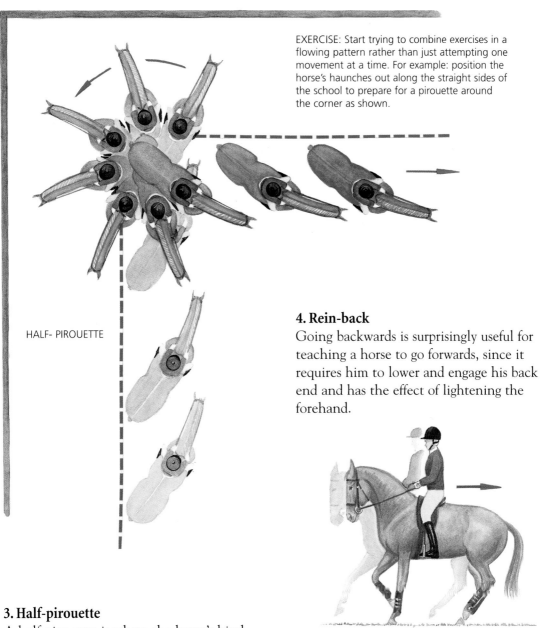

EXERCISE: Start trying to combine exercises in a flowing pattern rather than just attempting one movement at a time. For example: position the horse's haunches out along the straight sides of the school to prepare for a pirouette around the corner as shown.

HALF- PIROUETTE

4. Rein-back

Going backwards is surprisingly useful for teaching a horse to go forwards, since it requires him to lower and engage his back end and has the effect of lightening the forehand.

In rein-back, the rider must not pull the horse back using the hands, but must use the whole body to give the aid and use the legs to 'take' the horse back. Lighten (not lift) the seat bones in the saddle and bring the upper body forward by a small degree. Close both legs to ask the horse to begin stepping while closing the fingers around the rein to prevent forward activity.

3. Half-pirouette

A half-pirouette is where the horse's hind feet maintain a very slight forward step while the horse turns his forehand around them through 180° to change the rein. It can be done from halt or walk, and the horse is again bent slightly into the direction of travel.

21

RIDDEN EXERCISES: ADVANCED

You will notice that most of the more advanced exercises require a similar degree of bend from the horse and similar aids from the rider – they are essentially the same exercise, but in different places! In each case, the horse is bent in the direction of travel, which is far more demanding and the opposite of what he would naturally wish to do.

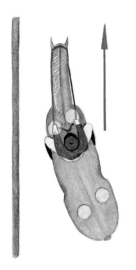

TRAVERS

The rider's shoulders should be parallel with the horse's shoulders and should look ahead between the horse's ears.

RENVERS

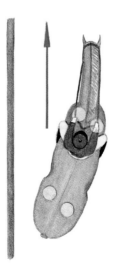

HALF-PASS

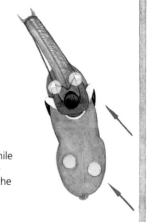

In half-pass to the left, the horse is bent slightly left while the right rein yields and the rider applies pressure with the right leg.

1. Half-pass
Like leg-yield, this is a forward and sideways stepping movement, but this time the horse is bent in the direction of travel, i.e. looking where he is going, which requires a greater degree of suppleness and coordination.

2. Travers
This is where the horse is in haunches-in but on three definite tracks, with the horse correctly and evenly bent through his whole body, as required for competition. The greater angle encourages engagement of the quarters (therefore preparing for collection) as well as flexion and lateral bend and is useful in preparation for the half-pass, which is a kind of 'travers on the move' across the school, rather than down the track.

3. Renvers
This is the 'counter-lesson' of travers, where the horse keeps his quarters to the wall and brings his forehand in off the track while continuing forward, bent in the direction of travel. It is often more difficult as there is no wall in front of the horse to keep him straight.

4. Full pirouette

Keeping the six classical training goals of the pyramid together is more of a challenge when riding a full pirouette than when attempting a half pirouette. Insufficient collection can result in the forehand being unable to take big steps in a proper rhythm, so the horse 'shuffles' around the circle.

5. Extension and collection

These are an advanced form of transition. Practising gait variations by asking the horse to shorten and lengthen his stride within the same gait to varying degrees (without losing rhythm, straightness, contact or impulsion), requires subtle riding and longitudinal suppleness in the horse.

FULL PIROUETTE

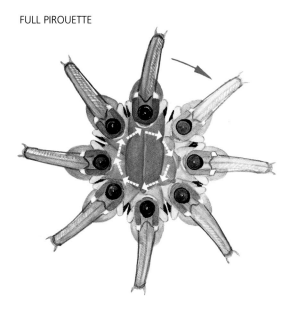

Although it may look as if it is done on the spot, a correct pirouette is not simply swinging the forehand around using the back legs as a pivot; the hind legs should maintain a very slight forward step and describe their own small circle.

The collected horse works in a much shorter frame. The most extreme form of collection is piaffe, where the horse 'trots on the spot'. In extended trot, the horse must lengthen his stride while maintaining balance and staying attentive to the rider's aids. Although the horse will cover the ground much more quickly, this should be a result of proper extending of the whole frame, rather than increased frequency of stride/ faster rhythm.

When is a movement classical?
There is constant debate over whether certain school movements are 'classical' in the purest sense, or just competition requirements.

Historically, any movement or technique that used to be commonly practised in past centuries (especially during the Renaissance and Baroque eras, the 'classical' period of dressage) has to be considered classical.

On the other hand, modern thinking suggests that any movement which has gymnastic value and helps to improve the gaits or to explain a certain aid to the horse, adheres to classical principles and can be considered classical.

The CLASSICAL CHECKLIST

However good your intentions, there usually comes a time when things aren't going according to plan, or you are frustrated by a lack of progress. Refer to this classical training checklist and it's likely that at least one point will strike you as relevant.

1. When analysing a problem, give the horse the benefit of the doubt, and start by looking at yourself critically. Remember that what might seem like lack of cooperation in the horse is often lack of understanding, and that humility is a characteristic of the classical horseman – you are the horse's trainer, and his behaviour is simply a reflection of your training. The horse also reflects other aspects of your personality at any given moment, such as your energy level or mood.

2. Go back to the training pyramid (page 11) and check that your foundations are strong. Have you properly established the base levels before moving on? If the horse has suffered any loss of confidence or setback he needs to go back and consolidate previous work.

3. Rule out the possibility that physical pain or discomfort are making the horse uncooperative. Get experts to check teeth, back, joints, muscles and the fit of your tack, especially the saddle. Scrutinise the horse's daily routine and diet to see if there is anything amiss.

4. Pay due attention to the horse's morale. The first signs of cooperation must be noticed and rewarded immediately. Set the horse up for success rather than pushing him to failure by asking a little less rather than a little more, stopping sooner rather than later. That way, you are putting yourself in a position where you can reward good behaviour and the horse will remain motivated by his own success. And **never** work your horse according to the clock. Make the length of your training session dependent on the form your animal is in that day.

5. If what you are doing isn't getting the message across, change it. Use other (ethical) tactics, techniques and exercises to communicate the lesson to the horse in a different way. This is what sets the complete classical horseman apart from a mere rider.

Finally, some words of wisdom from one of the great classical masters and former Director of the Spanish Riding School, Alois Podhajsky:

'When training his horse, the rider must repeat over and over again: "I have time".'